Adventures of Lil' Cub

Adventures of Lil' Cub

Lil' Cub Meets Bently

Story and Illustrations by Bruce E. Stratton

Computer Graphics Support by: Gary L. Hull

Copyright © 2025 by Bruce E. Stratton.

All rights reserved. No part of this publication may be reproduced, distributed, or transmitted in any form or by any electronic or mechanical means, including information storage and retrieval systems, without a prior written permission from the publisher, except by reviewers, who may quote brief passages in a review, and certain other noncommercial uses permitted by the copyright law.

Library of Congress Control Number: 2025902459

ISBN: 979-8-89228-001-3   (Paperback)
ISBN: 979-8-89228-000-6   (eBook)

Book Ordering Information:
Atticus Publishing
548 Market St PMB 70756
San Francisco, CA 94104
(888) 208-9296
info@atticuspublishing.com
www.atticuspublishing.com

Printed in the United States of America

HOW LIL' CUB GOT STARTED

I have always been able to draw and paint different pictures since i was a young boy. I used to draw cartoons of different types, but i could never make up a cartoon of my own. One day my daughter needed a cartoon strip for her art class in high school. She wanted to copy some of walt disney's characters, but i thought we should have an original character for her comic strip.

At first we thought of using a worm. I had drawn him in different positions with different expressions on his face. He was a cute little fella with a top hat cocked to one side of his head and he carried a cane. All this did not suit us so we tried other types of characters of which none pleased us. Then i thought we could draw a car or an airplane, and have them doing all sorts of actions.

So i started, first a few scribbles on my paper, then a few lines, a shape started to take place. A small airplane with large eyes, a big grin and flappy wings came to life at the end of my pencil lil' cub was created.

I would like to share the first story of lil' cub with you. It was created for my daughter and dedicated to all who are young and those who are young at heart.

BRUCE E. STRATTON

Other books written by Bruce E. Stratton:

Adventures of Lil' Cub: In "Mercy Flight"

Lil' Cub and Bently get Girlfriends, Cessi and Belle

Lil' Cub becomes a Detective

Lil' Cub visits a Space Shuttle

Little Cub Learns all about Hot Air Balloons

Lil' Cub Tries to Build a New Hanger.

ADVENTURES OF LIL' CUB

It is a bright sunny day at the Sunny Valley Airport and Lil' Cub is looking for something to do when he sees something down by the runway.

As Lil' Cub gets near what he saw, he begins to laugh, "Ha-Ha you're the funniest thing I ever saw! Ha-Ha." He laughed so hard that tears fell from his eyes, "What are you, anyway?" he asked.

"I am a Helicopter, and my name is Bently. And I am not funny, it's just that I am different then you. That's all." said Bently.

"Well, hello Bently, my name is Lil' Cub and I live here at Sunny Valley airport. What can helicopters do?" asked Lil' Cub.

"I can do a lot of things that you can't do," replied Bently.

Lil' Cub got excited and said, "Oh yeah? Like What?"

"Well, like I can fly straight up," said Bently as he turned his main rotor blades and went right up in the air.

"And I can fly straight down," said Bently as he returned to the ground.

"I can fly forward, backward, OR just hang in one place like this!" said Bently.

Lil' Cub was embarrassed, but he thought to himself, "I still think he looks funny."

Then Lil' Cub said to Bently, "Wow, I guess you aren't so funny after all."

"The way you can fly is just great, but there are some things I can do that you can't."

"Like what?" asked Bently.

"I can fly a loop-de-loop." Says Lil' Cub
as he flies up and around.

ADVENTURES OF LIL' CUB

"I can fly upside down as well!"

"Oh," said Bently. "I can't do that,
but what else can you do?"

"I can do barrel rolls too!" said Lil' Cub as he twisted and turned his way through the air. "And I can fly upside down." Said Lil' Cub as he gave Bently a big grin.

"Wow" said Bently. "I guess we both do different things."

"Maybe we both have special things we can do, and maybe that's why we are different." Stated Lil' Cub.

Bently said, "Helicopters help people fight forest fires by dropping water on the fire, where firefighting equipment can't go."

Lil' Cub said, "Small airplanes look for people who are lost in wild areas, so they can be rescued, they can fly slow and low."

It was Bentley's turn. "Helicopters rescue people at sea because we can hang in one place and pick them out of the water."

Lil Cub said," I have delivered special medicine that was needed quickly to save lives, and the Big Airplanes couldn't fly because of fog and bad weather."

Bently smiled, "Large helicopters lift logs from lumber camps to the saw mill to make lumber to build houses and wooden things."

"And," Bently continued, helicopters are also used to carry supplies to the top of new buildings that are being built."

"And," Bently said, "Helicopters take sick and injured people to the hospital fast, because they can land without the need of a runway."

Lil' Cub spoke up and said, "Some small planes have pontoons on them so they can land on lakes or rivers and deliver supplies and medicine to remote wild areas."

"Well, it seems we both can do many things when there is trouble and we are needed to help out." Said Bently.

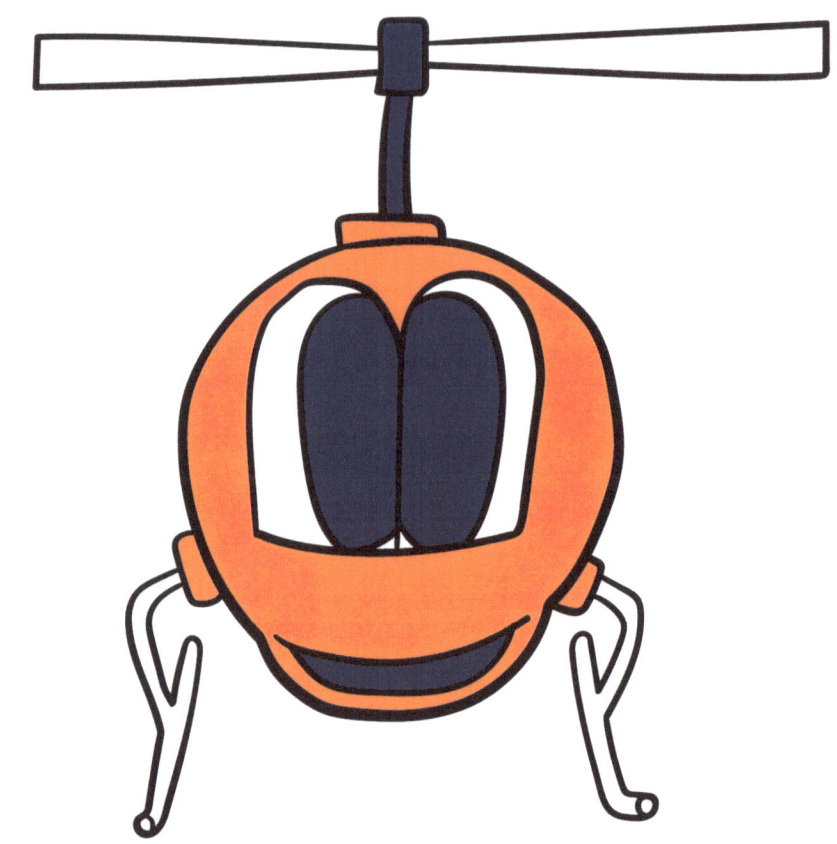

"Yes," said Lil' Cub, "And even though we are different, I would like you to be my friend. We could do many fun things together too!"

Just as they were sharing a warm moment, an urgent call came over the airport radio: a little bird was tangled in a tree near the runway and couldn't fly down!

Lil' Cub was eager to help. He flew up to the tree but quickly realized he couldn't get close enough without risking his wings on the branches. He turned to Bently, eyes wide. "Bently! You can hover right by the tree without getting tangled. Can you help the little bird?"

Bently gave a confident nod, his rotors spinning as he gently hovered beside the tree. Carefully, he used his rotor blades to blow the leaves aside, guiding the little bird free from the branches.

The grateful bird fluttered down, chirping a sweet "thank you" to both friends.

Lil' Cub and Bently fly off together as the best of friends to have many adventures and a friendship that will last forever.

Side by side, they glided through the clouds, their laughter echoing through the air as they flew off to explore new places, help others, and share a friendship as boundless as the sky itself.

Lil' Cub Says:-
- Don't make fun of things you don't understand.
- Things aren't always as funny as they look!

Plane facts:

Helicopters do not have wings. They have vanes or rotor blades. The small rotor on top picks up the craft and makes it move up, down, forward, backward or stay in one place! Helicopters are also called Rotor Crafts

Don't make fun of things you don't understand.

Things aren't always as funny as they look !

Helicopters do not have wings. They have vanes or rotor blades.

The small rotor at the rear keeps the craft from spinning.

The large rotor on top picks up the craft and makes it move up, down, forward, backward or stay in one place !

Helicopters are also called Rotor Crafts.

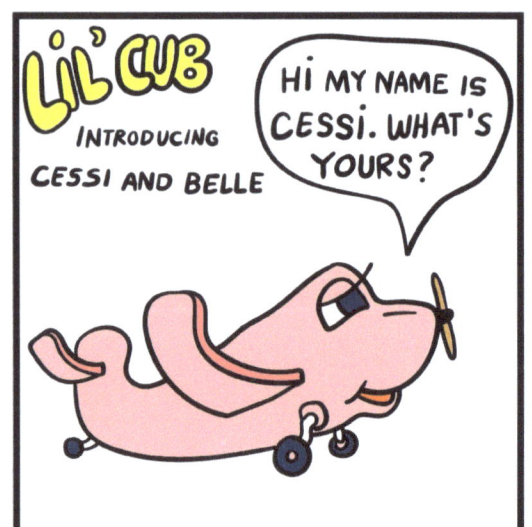

www.ingramcontent.com/pod-product-compliance
Lightning Source LLC
LaVergne TN
LVHW070441070526
838199LV00036B/675